Coloring Your Way to Serenity and Strength

Welcome to "Yoga Dudes: Coloring Your Way to Serenity and Strength."

This coloring book is designed for men who practice yoga, and who want to deepen their practice in a fun and engaging way.

Yoga is a practice that can bring both physical and mental benefits, and this coloring book is intended to support and enhance those benefits.

As you color in the designs, you can focus your mind, calm your breathing, and tap into your creativity. You may find that coloring helps you to access a deeper state of relaxation, or to process thoughts and emotions that have been difficult to express.

The designs in this book are inspired by the practice of yoga, and are intended to help you connect with different aspects of the practice.

Some of the designs feature poses, such as the warrior or the tree pose, while others incorporate symbols like the lotus flower or the om symbol.

We hope that this book will be a tool for you to deepen your practice, and to find greater peace, strength, and serenity in your life.

Remember, there are no right or wrong ways to color - simply enjoy the process and let your creativity flow.

Namaste.